The Watchman

by Linda Adwoa Aidoo

The Watchman

Trilogy Christian Publishers A Wholly Owned Subsidary of Trinity Broadcasting Network

2442 Michelle Drive Tustin, CA 92780

Copyright © 2023 by Linda Adwoa Aidoo

Rights Department, 2442 Michelle Drive, Tustin, CA 92780.

Trilogy Christian Publishing/TBN and colophon are trademarks of Trinity Broadcasting Network.

Cover design by: Grant Swank

For information about special discounts for bulk purchases, please contact Trilogy Christian Publishing.

Trilogy Disclaimer: The views and content expressed in this book are those of the author and may not necessarily reflect the views and doctrine of Trilogy Christian Publishing or the Trinity Broadcasting Network.

Manufactured in the United States of America

10 9 8 7 6 5 4 3 2 1

Library of Congress Cataloging-in-Publication Data is available.

ISBN: 978-1-63769-992-8

E-ISBN: 978-1-63769-993-5

Table of Contents

Dedication/Acknowledgements

I would like to dedicate this book first to my Lord and my God, who, by His mercy and grace, chose me for this assignment through a prophetic vision long ago, even while I was still a baby Christian in my faith. I would like to bless and honor the man (Mr. William Mintah Hayford), through whom the Lord gave this prophetic vision concerning me and the title of the book many years ago. This vivid vision was truly set for an appointed time; it has tarried, but the Lord Jesus Christ Himself has made it possible to be fulfilled now, for such a time as this, and we are grateful.

A special thank you to my biological parents (Dr. Anthony Yaw Aidoo and Mrs. Agnes Aidoo) and my siblings for their constant love, encouragement, and for supporting me along this journey and in all that I do.

This book would not have become a reality without the encouragement, prayers, and support of my spiritual parents, Apostle Frank Asirifi and Mrs. Philomina Asirifi. I thank Apostle for initially going through my rough draft and scribbles and offering me great advice.

I would like to honor and render my sincerest thanks to my Regional Head of New England Region, Apostle & Mrs. Sampson Ofori Yiadom, for their prayers and encouragement. And to my District Pastor and his wife, Rev. & Mrs. Hayford Gyampoh, for their prayers, love, and constant encouragement! To my Presiding Elder & members of my church family and local presbytery, thank you all for supporting me in my spiritual growth.

To my dear spiritual mother, Deaconess Mrs. Joyce Attakora: Mommy, thank you for your extraordinary prayers, support, and encouragement, especially during my moments of enormous self-doubt.

To my spiritual mother, Mrs. Maureen Briggeman: What a great woman of Intercessor you are! Thank you for loving me and standing in the gap for me all these years.

To all my close-knit support system of fathers and mothers of faith, friends, sisters, brothers, uncles and aunties, who held me accountable to fulfilling this call from the Lord through your prayers and words of encouragement, God richly bless you, I honor and celebrate each one of you! To all my spiritual leaders, anyone who has been a part of my spiritual journey with the Lord in one way or the other, please know that you're an integral part of fulling this assignment from our Lord Jesus Christ. *The Call of the Watchman,* **in this end time, is an urgent call we must all answer on a daily basis.**

Spiritual watchmen are people God has called and commissioned in this end time, strategically positioned by God to carry out divine assignments wherever they find themselves.

Chapter 1

The Identity of a Watchman

A watchman can mean so many things to different people. To some, it means people who identify themselves as neighborhood watchmen. In some other cultures, it means the person you hire as a guard or security person for your home, business or school, or any type of organization.

At least from my native land, Ghana, the second definition describes who a watchman is perfectly. We had great watchmen at our schools who were responsible for opening and shutting our school gates and making sure there was enough security at our school gates. And because the school I was fortunate to attend as a little girl was an all-girls boarding school, their presence at our school gates was highly important. They took their jobs seriously and interrogated every single person coming in and out of the gates of the school.

Here in America, we call them security guards. We meet them in so many places; from our workplaces to our banks, we find them doing their work. Their presence can make us feel a bit protected whenever we see them. I personally feel a bit secure and happy whenever I walk to my local bank and a security guard greets me.

Watchmen are highly significant in the work that they do. In the same way, there are some spiritual watchmen as well in the Kingdom of God. They are people God has called and commissioned in this end time, strategically positioned by God to carry out divine assignments wherever they find themselves.

Perhaps, you are among this great army of people God identifies as a watchman, and yet you don't even know it. Or maybe you are truly far from being classified as one. Whatever your take on this is, it is my humble and yet fervent prayer that by the time we finish reading, we will be able to say to God, "Help me to be a watchman wherever I find myself, anytime, anywhere for your glory, and your Kingdom."

Watchmen in the Kingdom of God take personal responsibility of drawing souls unto the Kingdom of God.

Chapter 2

The Divine Assignment of Spiritual Watchmen in Everyday Life

Spiritual watchmen are born-again Christians, spirit-filled believers, and everyday people who keep watch over the souls of people. They are people who, first of all, know God, have a deep personal relationship with God, and are willing to share the saving knowledge of Christ by faith through *grace and love* with others, through any means or platforms that God makes available unto them.

Watchmen in the Kingdom of God take personal responsibility of drawing souls unto the Kingdom of God. They take the great commission from our Lord Jesus Christ personally and do whatever they can to be a great witness of Christ to others. They live with that consciousness every day and look for ways to make the love of Christ known to others.

Watchmen are in tune with the Spirit of God and take time to hear from God so that they can deliver what they have heard, studied, or gleaned from the Word of God to others.

There are all kinds of watchmen in both the Old and New Testaments.

Old Testament watchmen were usually people who were essentially the eyes and ears of the reigning king. They kept watch and reported anything suspicious or posing as a threat to the nation or the security of the king to him so that the king could be alert and know how to strategize on what to do or decisions to take.

In our day and our time, they would probably be like FBI/CIA agents to the president.

Their job is extremely important! The whole nation needs them in matters relating to the security of the nation.

And then there were some prophets that God used to either guard a city or nation and to deliver a message from the Lord to a particular people. They were essentially God's watchmen.

The Prophet Ezekiel was one of such great watchmen that God called, ordained, or mandated to carry out such divine tasks. Ezekiel chapter 3, verse 17 says:

> *Son of man, I have made thee a watchman unto the house of Israel: therefore hear the word at my mouth, and give them warning from me.*
>
> Ezekiel 3:17 (KJV)

Watchmen sounded the alarm to let the king and everyone know that there was an impending danger so that people could take cover.

Ezekiel as a watchman was to sound the alarm of repentance so that the people of God could turn from their wicked ways and follow the ways of Jehovah God.

> *Again the word of the Lord came unto me, saying, Son of man, speak to the children of thy people, and say unto them, When I bring the sword upon a land, if the people of the land take a man of their coasts, and set him for their watchman: If when he seeth the sword come upon the land,*

he blow the trumpet, and warn the people; Then whosoever heareth the sound of the trumpet, and taketh not warning; if the sword come, and take him away, his blood shall be upon his own head. He heard the sound of the trumpet, and took not warning; his blood shall be upon him. But he that taketh warning shall deliver his soul. But if the watchman see the sword come, and blow not the trumpet, and the people be not warned; if the sword come, and take any person from among them, he is taken away in his iniquity; but his blood will I require at the watchman's hand. So thou, O son of man, I have set thee a watchman unto the house of Israel; therefore thou shalt hear the word at my mouth, and warn them from me. [...]

Say unto them, As I live, saith the Lord God, I have no pleasure in the death of the wicked; but that the wicked turn from his way and live: turn ye, turn ye from your evil ways; for why will ye die, O house of Israel?

Ezekiel 33: 1–7, 11 (KJV)

The Prophet Ezekiel's assignment during his day is definitely not far from us believers of Jesus Christ.

Each of us is here on an assignment! We are not here by accident! God has intentionally placed us here for a reason. We are the new watchmen, watchwomen, watch ladies, watch boys and watch girls that God is counting on in this end time.

We are the very ones that our Lord Jesus Christ came to die for, shed his blood for, suffered for, and resurrected for. We are the ones that Christ Jesus has commissioned!

We are the carriers of the Great Commission, bearers of the true good news, the true Gospel, the unadulterated and undiluted Word of God. We, who are born again and have an authentic relationship with the Lord Jesus, carry the Holy Spirit. Our body is the temple of the Holy Spirit.

God has a message for this world that He wants to deliver through you. God has a divine word for those around you, where He has placed you, your sphere of influence, your workplace, your family, children, friends, school, college campus, neighborhood, in the marketplace, wherever you find yourself as you read this book, know that you are the representation of Christ there.

You are responsible for the souls of the people around you. Most of us Christians or believers of today have completely lost sight of this. We have forgotten the true meaning of who the church is: the body of Christ Jesus, meaning we are His hands, feet, mouth, and eyes everywhere we find ourselves.

One of our principal goals is to draw souls unto the Kingdom of God. But sadly, we have become a church with "blood on our hands."

> *When I say unto the wicked, O wicked man, thou shalt*
> *surely die; if thou dost not speak to warn the wicked from*
> *his way, that wicked man shall die in his iniquity; but his*
> *blood will I require at thine hand.*
>
> Ezekiel 33:8 (NKJV)

The church has a responsibility, a divine mandate to reach out to lost souls for the Kingdom of God. This mandate is on us as individuals and collectively as a group.

Just as we believe, claim, and personalize the promises of God to our benefit or advantage, we should, in the same manner, take being a witness of the Lord Jesus Christ personally.

We all need to be serious about it and not relegate it to only ordained ministers.

Wherever you find yourself right now, as you read, know that you're the Minister over there, we are all in ministry, one way or the other, and God is counting on us.

> *Son of man, I have made thee a watchman unto the house of Israel: therefore, hear the word at my mouth, and give them warning from me.*
>
> Ezekiel 3:17 (KJV)

God said to the Prophet Ezekiel, "*I have made thee a watchman.*"

This means God is the only one who calls us for a specific assignment; He ordained us for that, and when God truly appoints you for something, He definitely equips you with power, strength, boldness, utterance, the resources, both spiritually and physically. God provides the unction to function for His glory.

There are so many people out there claiming to be called or appointed by God, doing all kinds of things in the name of the Lord, but in reality, God has no part in it. They are not truly sent by God. As a result, they are deceiving many. There are "so-called" men of God all over the place who are people pleasers, attention seekers, validation seekers, popularity contest people, and sadly are out of sync with the Word of God.

They may be preaching, but they have no authentic word from the Lord. They are serving but for selfish ambitions, *self*-promotion. These kinds of people place a lot of emphasis on the elevation *of their spiritual gifts over the giver of the gift, who is God Himself.*

Manifesting the gifts of the Spirit without the preeminence of the love of God and the evidence of the fruit of the Spirit in our lives is dangerous to our spiritual growth. The reason being that gifts and calling of God are irrevocable (Romans 11:29). God doesn't take them back; however, we can operate in them to elevate the "self" or operate in them in the spirit of love to honor the Lord. This was what the Apostle Paul was trying to address in 1 Corinthians 13:1–13 and Galatians 5:22–23.

What God is calling us as watchmen to step into is to be grounded in the Spirit of God and with tangible evidence of the fruit of the Spirit in our lives. We are being called to step into a place where we not only manifest the gifts of the Holy Spirit, but our foundation and example is truly the Lord Jesus Christ, who is love personified. We are being called to step into a realm where our lives are infused with the love of God, and we are living it practically in addition to fully manifesting the gifts of the Spirit. When we are led by the Spirit in living and doing everything out of love and humility, Christ will be glorified, and "the self" will definitely be crucified.

Our step of obedience
to the voice of the Lord
has the potential to
unlock destinies and
ultimately, alter lives
for eternity.

Chapter 3

Watchmen Sound the Alarm for Repentance

A true watchman of God *"hears the Word at the mouth of the Lord"* and gives warning immediately.

Watchmen carry a message with a sense of urgency. It is a message of complete repentance. It is a message to seek after holiness, to seek after God. It is a message about salvation, grace, love, and the power of the Holy Spirit, but it is also a message about the justice and the impending judgment of God.

Watchmen preach about the unadulterated Word of God, the uncompromising life-changing Word of God. Watchmen are not afraid to proclaim the truth but are able to communicate the truth to both old and young. Watchmen sound the alarm regarding what the Lord has to say to His people, be it individually or to the masses.

Most messages from our pulpits are more motivational speeches to soothe the itching ears of our hearers rather than the sound Word from the Lord.

Messages that activate the convicting power of the Holy Spirit, pricking our hearts and leading us to repentance and experiencing the true love and move of God, have become extinct.

"All scripture is given by inspiration of God, and is profitable for doctrine, for reproof, for correction, for instruction in righteousness" (2 Timothy 3:16, KJV).

When the Word comes for correction and rebuke, let's not resort to defensiveness and judgmentalism, but in humility, fall on our knees before the King of kings and repent.

The church cannot just only preach about the "feel good" messages to hype people's emotions, after which they return to a place of emptiness—spiritually. When the message being preached is not backed by God and the Holy Spirit, it becomes void of the manifestation of the power of God.

If there was a time for true watchmen to wake up and sound the alarm or trumpet of repentance, that time is now. There is no time to delay because the truth of the matter is that none of us really know when the Lord Jesus Christ is going to appear for the second time.

None of us really know for sure when we are going to die or what is going to lead to that, which is why it is even more important for us as watchmen to make sure that with every opportunity that the Lord gives us with people, we make it a point to let them see Christ in us and preach about the Kingdom of God, the salvation message of Christ, and the need to turn away from sin and honor God with our lives each and every day.

Today's date, as I'm writing, is March 24, 2020. My time says 1:02 a.m. in the morning. And yes, I'm up writing what the Lord has laid on my heart.

During this season of this year, most of us can attest to the fact that life has been a very challenging time for everybody around the globe. Never in my life have I seen something like this happen on a global scale, a day and time in history when churches, schools, and businesses closed, all because of the spread of a deadly virus called coronavirus or COVID-19.

Fear and panic have gripped most people, precious lives perished at such an alarming rate in some parts of the world, and yet during this chaos, some of us turned solely to God for grace and strength.

During this season, some of us did a lot of soul-searching, prayed a lot, sought the face of the Lord through His Word, and some fasted. Whatever way we could connect to God, we sure did.

We all had so many lessons and perhaps revelations, encounters, and revelations from the Lord as we began to seek the face of God. But personally, one thing stuck up to me, and that was the fact that I realized had Jesus appeared during this time, I would still have had unfinished assignments that I personally believed the Lord wanted me to do for the Kingdom of God.

Part of this was due to the fact that I knew without a shadow of a doubt that the Lord was calling me to write and that through these writings, He was going to draw others into the Kingdom of God and strengthen the faith of others.

And yet, for some reason, I have for so many years felt inadequate to do this. For a very long time, I felt unqualified to handle this assignment, and I would even tell the Lord sometimes that perhaps other people would do a better job delivering this message better than me. Besides, I've not been to any Bible school and have no major social media presence or platforms. I would rather be a behind-the-scenes person than be in the forefront of things.

Well, these were some of my excuses...and they went on and on. My insecurities and fears were magnified in my head. And I'm sure as you read this today, you may also have your own game of excuses you have played with God for years, months, weeks, or days in regard to fulfilling your divine purpose.

Being it lack of faith, confidence, insecurity, or whatever yours may be, I pray that the Lord who has enabled me to write what you're reading right now will strengthen you and give you grace to step into your divine calling or assignment and manifest it to the glory of God.

Because the truth is each of us brings something unique to the table when it comes to the building of the church or Kingdom of God. We each hold something powerful, anointed, and ordained by the King of kings and the Lord of Lords to be used for His glory and purpose.

We all have a trumpet to sound to the hearing of all creation; the question is, are you going to sound yours, or are you going to walk away?

Time is of the essence, and the truth is tomorrow is never promised, so *we need to make a conscious effort to maximize "the precious gift of today."*

Our step of obedience to the voice of the Lord has the potential to unlock destinies and ultimately alter lives for eternity.

Watchmen are ambassadors of Christ! We represent the Kingdom of God; our citizenship is not just limited to our geographical locations, but it is in heaven.

Chapter 4

Watchmen Carry the Message of Reconciliation

God is reconciling men/women back to the original relationship with mankind through Christ (2 Corinthians 5:18–21).

The reason why God hasn't taken you to heaven yet or doesn't take us to heaven the moment we accept Him as our Lord and Savior is because He still has a work for us to do.

God is counting on you and me to help others to come to the saving knowledge of Christ, to restore others back to Him, to practically share the love of God in meaningful ways with our world.

One of the ultimate reasons why God sent His only-begotten Son, Jesus Christ, into the world is for us sinners to be restored to our heavenly Father, to have that Father and child relationship that existed in the garden of Eden back.

It was for us to enjoy the ever-constant presence of God each day, each moment, here on earth through the Holy Spirit eternally with the heavenly Father.

Our Lord Jesus Christ came to plug us back into a relationship with the Father God once again. It is just so we can live in a realm or atmosphere where we can commune freely with God without any barriers.

And so the truth is that we who are saved by grace, through faith, children of God who happens to be alive in this present age, are called upon for such a time as this to carry the good news to others so that they, too, can return home to their true spiritual Father, so that they, too, can be carriers of God almighty, walk in purpose, be part of the Kingdom work, and partake in all that the heavenly Father has made available freely to us.

Watchmen are ambassadors of Christ! We represent the Kingdom of God, our citizenship is not just limited to our geographical locations, but it is in heaven.

We operate with a Kingdom mindset! "For in him we live, and move, and have our being" (Acts 17:28, KJV). We are on a mission for God wherever we find ourselves. We are ambassadors sent by the King of kings and Lord of lords to live out the Kingdom principles right where we find ourselves today. And when we start living out and doing the work of ambassadors for Christ, the needed resources will be provided unto us.

God knows how to take care of His children who are on the field. God has never run out of resources or provision.

Let's be *intentional* about letting our lives represent Christ's saving grace, unconditional love of God, kindness and compassion of the Lord, the manifestation of the Spirit of God, and the evidence of the fruit of the Spirit in our lives.

Pray all kinds of prayer, pray in the spirit at all times, but *NEVER* PRAY outside of *THE WILL* OF GOD.

Chapter 5

Watchmen Stand in the Gap

God has always been looking for somebody to stand in the gap for His people. In every generation, there are men and women that God picks up and anoints them, prepares them, and makes them a *voice* in those generations. Throughout the Bible, we always see God doing this, raising men like Abraham, Isaac, Jacob, Joseph, Moses, Deborah, Ruth, Mary, Paul, Peter, and many others. In our dispensation, we have heard and seen or read of great men and women like Billy Graham, Smith Wigglesworth, Kathryn Kuhlman, Archbishop Benson Idahosa, Reverend James McKeown, and so many others.

God has always been relentlessly looking for someone who will stand in the gap so that God can manifest His plans and purposes in the lives of His people. In Ezekiel 22:30 (KJV), the Lord says, "*And I sought for a man among them, that should make up the hedge, and stand in the gap before me for the land, that I should not destroy it: but I found none.*"

When the people of God went astray, and yet God wanted to bring deliverance to the people. He was searching for a human entity; through whom, He will accomplish this, but sadly, the Bible records here that God found none. As a result, God carried out His judgment against Jerusalem because there was no one to stand in the gap.

There are certain things that God will not do without divine partnership with man! Although He is an all-powerful God, there are times He chooses not to move until we partner with Him.

29

Abraham, as a watchman, stood in the gap for Lot when God revealed to him about His plans to destroy Sodom and Gomorrah. He negotiated several times with God to see if God would relent in destroying the people of Sodom and Gomorrah if ten people were found righteous. To which God assured him that He would not bring the impending judgment for the sake of the ten. Abraham did not speak again after the God's response, perhaps thinking that ten righteous people would be found. But as it turned out, that wasn't the case.

As a matter of fact, Lot and his family were preserved and saved from the destruction based on Abraham's intercession. The Bible says that Lot and his family were preserved because God remembered Abraham (Genesis 19:29, KJV).

Abraham stood in the gap of intercession for the people of Sodom and Gomorrah and for the sake of his nephew Lot and his family. As a believer, with full access to the Holy Spirit, the presence of God, the Word of God, grace of God, the wisdom, the love of God, and the ability to pray....who is God showing mercy to because of you? Whose life is being preserved for eternity because of what you allowed God to use you for on behalf of others? Who is being fed, clothed, encouraged, comforted, educated, mentored, and kept under the feet of Christ today because of your impact?

What do you have in your hands today that can work miracles before Pharaoh? What are your God-given gifts, talents, and skills that you can use to bless humanity and cause others to praise God because of you?

God is looking for people that He can display His manifold blessings through, both spiritually and physically, in this end time; the question is, would you be willing to say "yes" to God?

These are valid personal questions that we can all ask ourselves in the place of prayer.

The Prophet Habakkuk says, "I will stand upon my watch, and set me upon the tower, and will watch to see what he will say unto me, and what I shall answer when I am reproved" (Habakkuk 2:1, KJV).

This man knew the power of intercession, and so we see him petitioning God on behalf of the people of God. He was looking for answers from the *Lord*, not just for himself and his family, but he was seeking the face of God, looking for solutions regarding the challenges that the nation was experiencing.

He deliberately made up his mind to set himself apart and to diligently seek the face of God on behalf of God's people. He set himself upon his tower with full confidence that the *Lord* would meet up with him there in this place. He was there to watch (to wait on the *Lord* with all attentiveness), with the expectation to see (that is, to receive a clear vision from the Lord concerning what was happening). And then, he was also looking forward to receiving a sure word from the *Lord* before he said anything else regarding his complaints.

Habakkuk is an example of a watchman who comes to engage God actively on behalf of his nation with full confidence that, indeed, the *Lord* will be ready to release answers to him.

And true to his faith, his diligence, and his expectation, God also showed up big time with the surety of His Word for the nation regarding what was to come.

> *And the LORD answered me, and said, Write the vision, and make it plain upon tables, that he may run that readeth it. For the vision is yet for an appointed time, but at the end it shall speak, and not lie: though it tarry, wait for it; because it will surely come, it will not tarry.*
>
> Habakkuk 2:2–3 (KJV)

God proceeded with the rest of the full message to the prophet concerning what was to come in the subsequent verses of chapter 2.

When the Lord had finished speaking to him, he then lifted up a deep, sincere prayer of intercession in chapter 3, seeking for mercy on behalf of his people.

God is calling all believers to take our place as spiritual watchmen wherever we find ourselves. God is counting on us to show up with the same level of passion, perseverance, diligence, persistence, and fire of the Holy Spirit and ascend to our watch towers, a place where we can fellowship with God and seek the face of God for ourselves and others. For whatever space we find ourselves in, God is counting on us to be the ones who will release divine and practical solutions to the challenges of our day and time. We are to champion the course of lives with the spirit of excellence, integrity, and lasting impact in the lives of everyone we meet.

The truth is God is ready to meet the end-time watchmen who

want to actively engage with God, receive bigger visions, receive *rhema* word, receive understanding and wisdom from the presence of the Lord so that they can impact the world for Christ!

The Apostle Paul understood this so well that he wrote to Timothy about this.

> *I exhort therefore, that, first of all, supplications, prayers, intercessions, and giving of thanks, be made for all men;*
>
> *For kings, and for all that are in authority; that we may lead a quiet and peaceable life in all godliness and honesty.*
>
> *For this is good and acceptable in the sight of God our Savior;*
>
> *Who will have all men to be saved, and to come unto the knowledge of the truth.*
>
> *For there is one God, and one mediator between God and men, the man Christ Jesus;*
>
> *Who gave himself a ransom for all, to be testified in due time.*
>
> 1 Timothy 2:1–6 (KJV)

God is looking for believers to assume the role of watchmen daily so that prayer is not just limited to our personal fellowship and needs before God but that we step into a higher dimension of prayer, which is intercession for others, those in authority or leadership positions, families, and for nations.

When we come seeking for answers to God's agenda, kingdom

impact, national solutions, inventions, creativity, and business ideas beyond our personal selfish reasons to honor the Lord, I believe God will respond to us.

A call for every believer to rise as a spiritual watchman is a call we must all answer in our everyday lives, in this end time, in our own unique ways that God has called us to serve to glorify the Lord.

May it not be that when God is looking for someone to stand in the gap for our homes, workplaces, and social media, in this generation, we are nowhere to be found! When the Lord calls for people who are in an authentic relationship with Him, holiness, true worshippers in Spirit and in truth, ambassadors of the Most High God, prayer warriors, may we be found.

We bless God the Father that time and time again, when there was no qualified mediator between God and man, God Himself sent His Son to be the ultimate sacrifice and channel for us. The Lord Jesus Christ, our High Priest, became the ultimate intercessor between humanity and God Himself.

Intercession is one of the principal duties of a watchman. As important as it is, intercession isn't something you can easily do on your own. You will need grace from the Lord to stand and pray and believe God for answers.

> *Who is he that condemneth? It is Christ that died, yea rather, that is risen again, who is even at the right hand of God, who also maketh intercession for us.*
>
> Romans 8:34 (KJV)

The ministry of intercession is still one of the ministries that the Lord Jesus Christ continues to do for believers today. And so, as we take part in this ministry, we should know that we are doing exactly what the Lord wants us to do.

When we look closely at the ministry of our Lord Jesus Christ, with Him leaving His deity as fully God and coming to take on the form of human being, dying for us, and becoming the means by which we can be eternally restored to the heavenly Father, and then, currently forever interceding for us at the right hand of God, you know that He is the ultimate sacrifice, an epitome of a true intercessor in every bit of the word.

There is nothing the Lord is calling on us to do that He hasn't already done before. He is and remains our truest example in all things, and I'm glad He doesn't leave us to do things on our own, but rather He comes along with us, walking side by side with us daily.

One thing we should come to understand is that intercession is not just limited to prayer but that there are different aspects of it.

Intercession through prayer is an integral part of it. Thus, being able to pray according to the will of God on behalf of others, be it family, children, husband, wife, leaders, national leaders, or basically anyone in authority over us, spiritual leaders, intercession for nations, regions, or states, cities or towns, neighborhoods. Whatever or whoever the Lord lays on your heart to intercede for, you honor the Word and do so.

If the church returns to the ministry of intercession with the heart of the Lord, we will experience more of the move of God.

The Lord Jesus Christ, before He went to the cross, left us an example to emulate as watchmen. When Jesus went into the garden of Gethsemane to pray during one of the darkest moments of His life, He brought along the two sons of Zebedee (James and John) along with Peter so that they would keep watch with Him in prayer. At this place of prayer, Jesus went a few steps away from them to seek the face of the heavenly Father in prayer.

Sadly, when He returned, He found His three disciples, followers, *sleeping*.

> *...and saith unto Peter, What, could ye not watch with me one hour? Watch and pray, that ye enter not into temptation...*
>
> Matthew 26:40–41 (KJV)

At a point when Jesus expected His disciples to be in a position of prayer, a place of intercession with their closest friend, He found them asleep. The three disciples missed the opportunity to seek the face of the heavenly with the Son of God.

It is interesting how when the Lord came to the three, He called out Peter's name, even though James and John (the two sons of Zebedee) were with him. Peter, the rock upon which the Lord Jesus says He will build His church. Peter, the leader of the disciples, was also asleep and could not watch and pray for an hour.

Prayer is a divine mystery. Prayer is an invitation from divinity, where mere mortals partner with a divine God. It is a place where the spirit of the mortal man connects and intersects with the Spirit of God so that the divine will and purposes of God are manifested.

Prayer is an opportunity to fellowship with God in an intimate way. Mysteries in the realms of the Spirit are revealed, the will of God is enforced, the power of God is tapped into, atmospheres and destinies are shifted, battles are won, and strength is released to withstand temptations.

The place of prayer is where we exchange our will for the will of God, even if it goes against our wishes.

The most powerful place to be as a believer is a place of prayer! And the most powerful prayer we can ever pray along this Christian journey is "...*not as I will, but as thou wilt*" (Matthew 26:39, KJV).

Pray all kinds of prayer, pray in the spirit at all times, but *never pray outside of the will of God.* Seek for the heart and will of the Father always. This is the kind of prayer our Lord and master Jesus Christ is calling us to pray.

Praying for the will of God to be made manifest is the very kind of prayer that our Lord Jesus Christ Himself modeled for us. Surely, it was the will of the heavenly Father for Son to endure the cross for me and you. And the Son accepted the call to suffer for us, even though it wasn't easy.

The Lord Jesus Christ received the supernatural strength needed to carry the cross, endure its shame and pain, death, and finally, resurrection for us. Grace abounds for us in a place of prayer. It should be our first resort and not the last.

Watchmen stand in the gap as priests of the Lord (1 Peter 2:9).

*But ye are a chosen generation, a royal priesthood, a holy
nation, a peculiar people; that ye should shew forth the
praises of him who hath called you out of darkness into his
marvelous light.*

1 Peter 2:9 (KJV)

By the divine grace of our Lord Jesus Christ, we have been
called of a royal priesthood of the Most High God. We stand before
God and His people. We minister to God and receive from God in
the secret place so that we can all share what we have received with
others.

We must daily be found in the presence of the Lord before
anybody else. What we carry from the presence of the Lord is what
we give to others.

We have been anointed to proclaim the righteousness of God
and declare the mind of God!

When the Samaritan woman had an encounter with the Lord
Jesus Christ, she left her empty bucket at the well and went to call
everyone to Jesus. Her past as the woman in town who has had five
husbands did not intimidate her.

She exchanged her life story of brokenness and shame at the well
and became a treasured vessel through whom a whole town will come
and encounter the Messiah for themselves. Destinies were eternally
changed through the testimony of the Samaritan woman, and the
Lord longs to bring similar transformation and impact through our
lives as well. There may be an audience waiting on the side of the
town, city, state, home, school, or social media who longs to connect

meaningfully with the Lord; they will only come when we show up as spiritual watchmen willing to stand in the gap for them.

The "Elizabeth Effect"

When Elizabeth heard Mary's greeting, the baby leaped in her womb, and Elizabeth was filled with the Holy Spirit. In a loud voice she exclaimed: "Blessed are you among women and blessed is the child you will bear! But why am I so favored, that the mother of my Lord should come to me? As soon as the sound of your greeting reached my ears, the baby in my womb leaped for joy. Blessed is she who has believed that the Lord would fulfill his promises to her!"

Luke 1:41–44 (NIV)

The relationship between Elizabeth and Mary was profound. The lessons we can draw from their relationship are countless. These two women were both carrying prophetic destinies, each on their own, and yet their unity, support, honor, and mutual respect, regardless of their age, were just beautiful and yet powerful at the same time.

The generational gap difference between Mary, young lady who was about to birth out one of the most biggest and longest awaited prophecies, versus Elizabeth, an old woman who miraculously was also carrying her own God-ordained child marked out for exploits, did not stop the two of them from connecting with each other.

When Mary was visited by angel Gabriel, who was also the same angel who brought Elizabeth's miracle, Mary could have chosen not to go and visit her. After all, she believed everything the angel of the Lord told her. She could have come up with a million reasons why she didn't need to see Elizabeth, but instead, she paid her a visit anyways.

Mary sought Elizabeth out. Mary went looking for her "Elizabeth." Regardless of what you are carrying, what you are about to birth out, how big your goal or dream is, and how marvelous and authentic your God-given idea is, never underestimate the significance of an "Elizabeth."

They play a key role in ushering you to your next level of your Kingdom assignment. Your "Elizabeth" doesn't necessarily have to be a woman, but metaphorically, "Elizabeths" may come in the form of mentors, coaches, counselors, teachers, friends, aunties, uncles, sisters, brothers, mothers, fathers, pastors, leaders, etc. The most important thing is having the wisdom and discernment to identify who such people are. And God is so good that one way or the other, He finds ways to connect us to such people. Sometimes all that it takes is to see through the lens of humility to know that they are all around us in our everyday lives.

Who do you have standing in the gap for you? And who are you interceding for? Are you an "Elizabeth" or a "Mary"?

It matters who is interceding for you in prayer, who is laying hands on you, who is preaching to you, and who you surround yourself with. What you are feeding yourself with spiritually, emotionally, mentally, and socially matters!

Mary's greeting wasn't just an ordinary greeting; because she was pregnant with a God-given purpose and destiny, her greeting brought about a spiritual activation of the Holy Spirit within Elizabeth. Until Mary showed up in Elizabeth's home, her baby never leaped for such level of joy in her womb. Neither did Elizabeth ever prophesy under the inspiration of the Holy Spirit, all this while carrying her pregnancy.

The truth is when you're intentional about hanging around the right people and being in the right environment, connecting with the right people who are capable of helping you become all that God has created you to be, "the baby in your womb will leap for joy."

Meaning you will be motivated to dream bigger and be better, and you will have your mindset shift leading to positive transformation and achieving greater results. An "Elizabeth" is filled with the Holy Spirit; therefore, speaks life and hope, confirms and affirms what God has called you to do. Never fails to speak a blessing over you and what God is going to use to you to accomplish and birth out. An "Elizabeth" is never intimidated by your Kingdom assignment and whether or not your assignment may be far greater than what they themselves are bringing forth.

Because they are led by the Holy Spirit, they are happy to see you win, thrive, learn, equipped, encouraged, and successfully launch out to be all that God has said about your life!

Elizabeth knew Mary was going to give birth to the Lord Jesus Christ, who would end up becoming her very own Savior, her Messiah, her Lord. And she was going to give birth to John the Baptist, who was to announce Mary's baby boy to the whole world. Because both women were filled with the Holy Spirit, there were mutual respect, honor, humility, and celebration of each other's Kingdom assignment.

If we can properly identify ourselves as either a Mary or an Elizabeth, it will change the way we stand in the gap for others. We will be more intentional about it.

I'm eternally grateful to God for being so kind and merciful in connecting me with "Elizabeths," whose prayers, encouragement, love, words of eternal hope and wise counsel have kept me under the feet of the Lord Jesus Christ, irrespective of all the raging storms I have faced in this life.

The trajectory of my life would have drastically shifted on a negative note if not for the grace and mercy of God, who made these connections possible. I stand so tall on the shoulders of many "Elizabeths," both spiritually, and also while going through school, and even in my professional career. Looking back, I see the hand of the Lord strategically placing each of these people in my life to create a transformational shift, although I didn't always fully understand it back then as much as I do now.

Many of these wonderful people have travailed in the presence of the Lord for me on so many occasions. Some prayed for my complete healing and restoration from brain injury as a result of a car accident. To God alone be all the glory forever! I honor and celebrate one of my spiritual fathers and his wife, who labored intensely in prayer for me during this season and continue to do so even to date.

One particular mom of mine in the faith has been praying and encouraging me through hand-written notes, letters, and cards that she has mailed to me for over ten good years now! Her notes and letters are so encouraging and Holy Spirit-filled I literally carry them in my handbags.

Another mother of mine who wears so many leadership hats simply considers me as her daughter, and I love and honor her as a mom. Not only has she blessed me with wise counsel, encouragement, fervent prayers, and practical wisdom, but she is one of the moms on whose shoulders I have cried on so many occasions, besides my biological mom's arms. She is just intentional about providing me with that safe space.

For privacy's sake, I had to withhold names, but essentially the point I'm trying to make is that we all have what it takes to be intentional about being a blessing to the lives of people God puts in our path on a regular basis.

These are everyday believers who are practically spearheading the call of a watchman in their daily lives, at different capacities, as the Spirit of God leads them.

Scripture says in 1 Peter 4:10 we should use whatever gift we have received to serve others. So whatever yours is, be sure to use it to stand in the gap for others and to bless humanity.

The overflow
experience and
blessings of God await
us when we show up in
total obedience &
dependence on God.

Chapter 6

Watchmen Depend on God

Except the Lord build the house, they labor in vain that build it: except the Lord keep the city, the watchman waketh but in vain.

Psalm 127:1 (KJV)

It is imperative that every watchman depends solely on God and God alone. Because apart from Him, there is nothing we can do.

No matter how much you preach the true Gospel to a lost soul, the ultimate conviction comes from the Spirit of God. No matter how much you intercede in prayers for anybody in any situation, the ultimate answer comes from our one and only sovereign God.

Practically, we also depend on God for divine direction and which steps to take at any point in time. When we partner with God, we allow Him to order our footsteps daily. We seek to obey Him and do what He wants us to do, even if it makes us naturally uncomfortable.

This is the only way we can be sure of not laboring in vain. When the Spirit of God takes precedence in everything we do, the bottom line is success in the sight of God, knowing that the ultimate impact is eternal impact because God is involved. Just like when Peter and his fishermen friends had fished all night long and caught nothing. These men were professionals, experts at their trade or careers! These men were good at fishing. And yet when Peter humbled himself and listened to the divine instructions from the Lord Jesus Christ and cast his net one more time at the same place, he caught nothing. He had an overflow when he allowed the Lord to direct him.

There is an overflowing waiting for us at the other side of our total dependence on God. There is an overflow at the side of obedience to the Word of God, persistence in our obedience to try one more time the very thing that we have failed at for so many years/times.

God may be calling some of us to revisit some divine assignments that we may have given up on for whatever reason. No matter how hopeless it may seem, let's give it one more try this time. Some of us need to go back to extending love to some of our wayward children, spouses, or other family members. For some of us, revisit a business idea you know the Lord gave you to pursue. For some of us, it may be a ministry we have neglected, and for some others, it may be perhaps waking up early or at night to pray for your children, spouses, family, or church. Whatever yours might be, let's pick up our nets one more time and cast them into the deep.

Casting our nets to the "*deep*" of prayer, fasting, studying the Word, evangelizing, the *deep* of strategizing, the deep of going the extra mile, the deep of dwelling a bit more in the secret place of the Lord. The *deep* of becoming more *self-less*, reaching out to others with the love of God, and putting others' needs above yours for the first time in your life.

There is a net-breaking blessing waiting for us, generational blessings, the level of blessings you know you cannot help but signal to others to come and be blessed also. The Ephesians 3:20 kind of blessings. Abundantly, exceedingly, beyond all we can ask or imagine.

Watchmen, partner with God, depend on Him, and you will never regret! He is faithful in all His ways.

We must see the lost and the hurting through the lens of Christ's compassion and desperate longing for each soul to be saved.

Chapter 7

Leaders as Watchmen

All believers are watchmen; however, church leaders, in particular, have a higher mandate or accountability. Hebrews 13:17 says it beautifully. Leaders are tasked with the highest responsibility of keeping watch over the lives of people entrusted into their hands. They answer to the highest level of authority on earth and also in heaven, who is God Himself, the judge of all mankind, the only true God who knows all and sees all, and that nothing is absolutely hidden from Him, whether things are done or said in secret or in broad daylight.

But practically speaking, just what does it mean for church or spiritual leaders to keep watch over the people that they lead?

Starting from whatever sphere of leadership influences the Lord Jesus Christ has entrusted into your hands, you're first and foremost expected to *please the Lord in all your ways.* Meaning making sure that you yourself are in the right standing with God the Father as far as your personal relationship is concerned.

Once your relationship with the Lord is intact, that is when you draw strength from the Lord by pointing others to this same Christ Jesus that you believe in.

Essentially this is a daily journey we take with the person and power of the Holy Spirit and grace from the Lord. We must start by sharing the love of Christ to a dying and perishing world in search of peace, hope, and love. It is important that we practice intentional evangelism, where we reach out to people regardless of who they are. We must be moved by a deeper sense of compassion for the hurting and the lost. Matthew 9:36 (NKJV) says, "But when He saw the multitudes, He was moved with compassion for them, because they were weary and scattered, like sheep having no shepherd." The Lord Jesus Christ, our Master, was often moved by compassion to reach out to people who needed Him the most. When our hearts are filled with compassion first for the lost and the needy, Christ is revealed and experienced through our outreaches.

Spiritual leaders must see the lost and the hurting through the lens of Christ's compassion and desperate longing for each soul we come into contact with or are capable of reaching.

This is where leaders begin to see the way Christ sees, go where Christ would go, sacrifice, and make every effort through the enabling power of the Holy Ghost to draw others to God through effective and intentional evangelism/discipleship, tangible acts of love and way of life to bless others, and most of all constant intercession in prayer.

The work is not about inviting believers already saved to come and be entertained and listen to feel-good, motivational messages every week while people leave empty, confused, disconnected, and spiritually bound, some still not even saved or have no relationship with Jesus Christ.

The Lord Jesus Christ is calling out to the body of Christ to a place of the highest level of spiritual priority, and that is to reach out to a dying world with the eternal word of life, grace, and love. Our shepherds in the body of Christ can no longer pride themselves on religiously keeping statistics of large attendance, memberships, and overflow, while some of these members are in spiritual confusion and do not confidently have a solid foundation in the basic elements of their faith and are easily tossed to and fro by every wind of teachings and prophetic manipulations.

When the true watchmen of the church shift our focus to pleasing the Lord by being carriers of the grace and love of God and fulfilling the great commission, we step into a place of divine alignment to the will and priority of God.

There is a dying world of people and multitudes all around us, most of them don't look and speak like us or live like us, but we are called to reach out to everyone with the eternal love of Christ.

We are the spiritual
firemen and women on
divine assignment for
the Most High God.
There is a sense of
urgency to the calling
of the watchmen.

Chapter 8

The Rescue Mission

"Be merciful to those who doubt; save others by snatching them from the fire; to others show mercy, mixed with fear—hating even the clothing stained by corrupted flesh" (Jude 1:22–23, NIV).

Imagine seeing your house or your neighbor's house on a blazing fire with people who are precious to you inside. Then you stand watching, and literally, you just decide to walk away, do something to entertain yourself, go about your normal day, and literally do nothing about it. Although you have an option to call for 911 for firemen to be dispatched, you have the option of crying out to other neighbors for help, and again you stand and make no move; you do not reach out for any level of help for loved ones who are trapped inside this burning house. Sadly, your lack of concern for people perishing in this house set on fire ultimately leads to the death of many precious souls.

You see, in real life, none of us will act this way! There is no way a normal person will stand aloof while their home burns without reaching out for some sort of help. Neither will neighbors and even total strangers given the same scenario will just pull out their cellphone devices and record without calling for assistance.

The truth is we don't think about souls we come across the same way we think about people who are trapped inside the burning house. Regardless of whether we know them personally or not, we just leave them in this spiritual "fire." Some are our own family members, friends, and total strangers we don't even know, and yet, although we have what it takes to reach out to them with the Gospel in one way or the other, we just keep to ourselves undisturbed.

We have become so comfortable with letting some people play with fires of sin. Some folks are held captive in the crutches of the enemy, whereas others are in the fire of ignorance. We have what it takes to be the ones to call for fire service men to be deployed to the rescue of those who are in danger. Most importantly, we have been equipped and positioned by God to stop the fire and bring relief to everyone experiencing any form of danger. *We are the spiritual firemen and women on divine assignment for the high God. There is a sense of urgency to the calling of the watchmen.*

Time is of the essence, both the rescuer and those who need to be rescued. Our tool or weapon for quenching the fire of sin is the Gospel of Jesus Christ. Our fire-extinguishing tools are to genuinely extend love, forgiveness, grace, and kindness in the same manner that the Lord God Himself has lavished on each of us. Our code of conduct is based on one solid standard: *Christ Jesus*, Him, and Him alone.

Whatever God has called you to accomplish on earth has a timeline to it. We must be people who understand the times and seasons we are in and what we ought to do—like the sons of Issachar were known for—so that we can make the most of every opportunity that the Lord Jesus Christ gives to us.

Because watchmen are on a rescue mission, they cannot be silent. They need to blow their "trumpets."

The enemy is always after *treasures* in our homes; he comes after the royal priesthood of God, the chosen people of God, a holy nation, a people set apart for such a time as this.

Chapter 9

Be the Spiritual Watchman in Your Home

The thief does not come except to steal, and to kill, and to destroy. I have come that they may have life, and that they may have it more abundantly.

John 10:10 (KJV)

The above scripture was the words from Jesus. He perfectly described that the three-major agenda of a thief is first to steal, kill, and destroy.

Usually, a thief will most likely not come to your house or property if he knows that you are wide awake with FBI and military personnel in your home. You see, a robber will not dare to enter such a home to steal anything because, obviously, the robbery operation will not be successful, and so this thief will not waste his or her time.

"To Steal." The reason why the enemy of our souls can come in and carry out his number one purpose in our lives is due to the fact that we are unguarded in the Spirit. When you have no covering in the Spirit, you're basically susceptible to anything. What is this covering? This is the covering of Christ as your ultimate head. We need to put on every single one of the armor of the Lord so that we can be fully on guard when the devil decides to come into our homes to steal, kill, and destroy.

Starting with the helmet of salvation, which protects our head, not just the physical head per se, but essentially our mind and emotions. Our salvation comes from the Lord Jesus Christ, who is the head of the church—individual believers like me and you. It is imperative that we stay connected to our spiritual head who is Christ Jesus, who embodies our salvation.

When we intentionally remind ourselves of our head being protected by the divine helmet of Christ's salvation, we can then also be reminded through the Holy Spirit, who constantly bears witness with our spirits, that we are indeed children of God and part of God's loving family.

As a result, our minds should be filled with Christ Himself. So much so that when the enemy tries to come in unexpectedly to try to steal what we know and believe to be the truth of God's Word in our minds, we can stand firm and remind him who we are and whose we are, children of the Most of High God, who stand on the shoulders of what our Lord Jesus Christ has already fought and accomplished for us, and resist him.

This is where we stand firm and take every thought of lies and deceptions from the enemy thrown at us and nullify it completely by the powerful Word of the Lord and by prayer.

This is where we stand with power and authority given to us by Christ and silence every voice of accusations from the enemy, every voice of anxiety, hopelessness, depression, fear, intimidation, and insecurity. This is where we counteract every deception with the unchanging Word and power of God.

The truth of the matter is if the enemy who pushes lies into our minds doesn't succeed in coming in *to steal—that is, coming to mess up*

*with us when not alert or guarded—he will not be able to move on to the
next level of his assignment, and that is to kill and ultimately destroy.*

This is the reason why believers need to wake up, be on guard,
and be the true spiritual watchmen wherever God has placed us. If
we can stay alert, be watchful in the Spirit, Word, prayer, evangelism,
and discipleship, and take our rightful positions in this world, a lot of
the enemy's agenda will be fruitless!

If we wake up and live truthfully and extend the unconditional
love, mercy, grace, and forgiveness that God has lavished on us to
those who don't deserve it, we will block the enemy from coming
into our hearts to sow any seeds of bitterness, unforgiveness, pride,
fear in our lives.

If believers wake up to the truth of the heartbeat of God for every
person they see—Christians and non-Christians, members of your
denomination, and non-members—our hearts will begin to beat for
salvation of everyone we come into contact with.

This is the time that believers need to wake up and stop fighting
for church membership, mere church attendance, denominational
allegiance, breakout from the trap of religion, which produces
spiritual arrogance like that of the Pharisees who looked down on
anyone who was not part of their sect or church and love with the
heart of God.

Time is running out. We must wake up, watchmen, and run with
the one and only one agenda, *the Kingdom agenda*, and nothing else.

Believers must wake up and work together hand in hand in the
spirit of love regardless of our denominational differences.

May the true spiritual watchmen of the Most High God wake up from our sleep of ignorance, legalism, and fear of man and know that we are called to walk in a deeper love and unity rooted in Christ. We extend the love of God to each other not because we fellowship together in the same local church or denomination, but because we are all part of the big family of Christ, and so, therefore, denominational barriers do not stop the flow of the love of God to each other.

When we rise up to be kingdom-minded people of God, the common denominator for us is the *agape* love of God. This love we have received from God by faith through grace is one, pure. This love is Christ personified. This love is timeless. This love is eternal, endless, and relentlessly pursues each of us each and every day, even the vilest offender among us.

When the true kingdom-minded watchmen wake up from the sin of *racism*, skin color will never be a barrier between one believer and another. Skin color will not decide if somebody is wrongly accused or killed in broad daylight, while on-lookers stand aloof and do nothing. The church of God, which is the light of the world, the salt of the earth, the carrier of true solution to racism, cannot continue to play politics, act in denial, and take no action at the frontlines but rather sit for unbelievers to take the active lead roles in crying out and demand justice for the oppressed and marginalized. The true spiritual watchmen of believers are summoned to be at the frontlines of eradicating any kind of sin, both spiritually and physically, whether *racism* or loss of lives of both old and young, not choosing one and then condoning the other.

When we become blinded to the truth of the Word of God and the sacredness of the unconditional love of Christ, our hearts become stolen by the enemy through the seed of hypocrisy, spiritual pride, and ignorance. This is a dangerous state sometimes believers find themselves in because, at this point, we become driven by our self-righteousness and self-justification of our sin rather than admitting humbly before the only true God that we need help living out the life of love for Him. This grand agenda of the devil *to steal* is mission accomplished where there is no presence and practical manifestation of the "*love*" of God.

Undeniably we can have the zeal, commitment, works, and giftings, but the absence of the *agape* love of God is a complete waste of our service to God. God is *love,* and therefore where we are unable to manifest this unconditional love to others, God Himself, the embodiment of *love*, is not there. We worship and serve God to please "the self," but God is not there, which is why the enemy can easily come in, sow discord, disunity, distrust, dishonor of leadership, and all kinds of sins you can think of. If we can put up the fence of the love of Christ, the enemy will definitely not be able to contend with us.

If we can manifest the love of God, no devil can stand a chance of stealing our hearts, killing and destroying us.

The enemy is also very clever and will not want to come to an empty home where there are no good treasures. Neither will he come and mess up with you and your family if you are ready for him. If you are already his prey, he won't need to put up with any resistance in the spirit or physically.

Nobody wants to come and steal your kitchen or bathroom trash. Why? Because it is so dirty, full of germs, and probably has no use to you except to dump it into a dumpster.

The enemy is always after treasures. He comes after the royal priesthood of God, the chosen people of God, a holy nation, a people set apart for such a time as this to fulfill Kingdom agenda. These are the very people that the enemy is after.

No wonder he went after the apostles in the olden days to make life hell for them just because they were preaching salvation to many people and bringing deliverances to many people. He went after Paul and Silas, Peter, James, etc.

And no wonder he is also after the treasure that God has put on the inside of us. But thanks be to God, who gives us victory through our Lord Jesus Christ. The victory has been won, and victory is ours.

When watchmen are alert and well-positioned to do battle, the enemy of our souls can be stopped in his tracks. For greater is He that is in us than he that is in the world.

Be intentional about clothing your children spiritually with unconditional love, prayer, and the Word of God.

Chapter 10

What Your Child Wears Counts

According to a report from the United States Department of Agriculture, "families might spend up to $1,280 annually on clothing, especially if you have tweens or teens. That's approximately 6 % of the total costs to raise a child." This was based on an article in 2018. I'm very much sure that this amount has gone up.

The truth is most parents do the very best that they can to make sure that their children are well taken care of. From the time they are babies to tweens and teenagers, the selection of clothes for the average kid is endless. And from the highly expensive name brands to the ones within the budget for most people, parents try as much as possible to make sure the children they love so dearly are properly clothed, not to mention the influx of electronic gadgets and toys.

But you see, for the love of your child, whether a baby, toddler, or teenager, the cost of clothes will never measure up to the cost of the love a parent has for his or her child. Moms and dads will sacrifice a lot to make sure that their kids have physical clothes to wear.

Your children may be wearing the best of clothes physically. For others, your kids probably have some highly expensive name brands and electronic gadgets. Nothing wrong with these; if you have the means to do so for your family, by all means, please do so.

But what if you were told that regardless of how much you worked so hard to clothe your precious kids, they are still not fully covered and protected? It is as if they are walking around with close to no clothes at all on them. Rain or shine. Winter or summer.

The truth is as bizarre as it may sound, some children have no proper covering spiritually. This makes them susceptible to all kinds of spiritual attacks of the enemy because they are spiritually exposed!

The way to make sure that children are fully protected or clothed spiritually is, first of all, through constant prayer and teaching them the Word of God. Invest quality time and prayer/fasting and teach them the Word of God.

There is a saying that "*it takes a village to raise a child.*"

If this saying holds some truth, then the sole responsibility does not fall just on biological parents but on the "village" as well, and that includes everybody, including you and me.

A few years ago, the Lord gave me a dream. In my dream, I saw two children of a dear friend of mine. I love these kids so dearly, and so I have become an aunty they adore. In my dream, I saw them playing in a particular place, but as I watched them closely, I saw that what they had on was brown paper-made clothes.

And so I asked myself why they were wearing clothes made of brown paper.

And the voice that I heard was: "This is how much prayer you cover them with." And then I woke up from my sleep.

I felt very sad and horrible when I woke up. I knew the Lord was speaking to me through this dream. I humbly repented before the Lord, and I knew then and then that I had to start serious intercession for these kids. And as the years went by, it has become one of the things I do every Saturday or Sunday morning, and that is to pray for all the kids in my local church family. Essentially every child in my family, and even those I do not know, I pray for them based on the leading of the Holy Spirit.

The question is, why didn't the Lord give this dream to the biological parents of these children but me? That was a question I was asking myself. I believe the Lord wanted to teach me the importance of assuming my role as a spiritual watchman, regardless of where I find myself. And that is to stand in the gap, in prayer for others, including children, and be among those who will be able to point these kids to the love of Jesus, whether through my actions or words.

If there was a time and season that the enemy was after your home, after the people who are so precious to you, which includes your precious children, it is now! It has been one of the key strategies of the enemy to come for our children. He has strategies, but how much are we prepared? He had a strategy to take out the Messiah when He was born, when He was just a baby. He was going to do it through the decree of *the king* at that time, who was Herod.

He also killed a lot of Hebrew boys at the time that Moses was born. There was another decree signed and issued by the king *in authority*, the Pharaoh, at the time.

These same wicked spirits that try to kill destinies are fully at work today but are masqueraded in various forms and wormed themselves into some homes and taken captives of the lives of precious children. Their identities are being switched spiritually. Not every child needs to be medicated. Some need fervent prayers and the unconditional *love* of God.

The Lord needs parents to wake up. He needs the church to wake up. The Lord needs church leaders who have no vision for children's ministry to wake up. The entire "village" needs to wake up, rise up in fervent prayer, and make sure that children are spiritually safe and secure starting from the home.

No loving mom or dad will send their child out in a cold winter without the appropriate winter clothes covering them in a minus ten degrees Fahrenheit weather. But for some reason, we are comfortable sending our kids to school without clothing them in prayer and power, without invoking the presence of the Lord to go with them, without feeding them with the Word of the Lord. Even if they can't understand, by faith, speak the Word of God over them. There is power in the Word of God.

Jesus said, "The words that I speak to you are spirit, and they are life" (John 6:63b, NKJV). And so, as we speak the Word, we are imparting the life, wisdom, and spirit of God into our children.

Jesus knew the importance of bringing children into the presence of the Lord. This was why He *did not permit His disciples* to prevent the children from coming to Him. He made room for the kids, children matter to the Lord, and they should matter to the rest of the body of Christ also.

> *Then little children were brought to Him that He might*
> *put His hands on them and pray, but the disciples rebuked*
> *them. But Jesus said, "Let the little children come to Me,*
> *and do not forbid them; for of such is the kingdom of*

heaven." And He laid His hands on them and departed from there.

Matthew 19:13–15 (NKJV)

When we have an opportunity to connect the hearts of children to the Lord, let's do it without any hesitation. In the scripture above, the "It takes a village to raise children" concept is highlighted because they did not even mention the names of the people who were bringing their children to the Lord for them to be blessed, protected, or covered.

That means we are all responsible to make this happen. We should be intentional about bringing children into the presence of the Lord. It doesn't necessarily have to be the responsibility of the biological parents alone.

The children of today cannot be future leaders of tomorrow if we are not willing to invest in their spiritual and physical growth. Just as we take it seriously to invest in the intellectual education of our kids, making sure they attend the proper schools and feed their physical bodies with balanced meals that nourish them physiologically, mentally, emotionally, and socially, we should not neglect our responsibility to make sure that they are spiritually fed, clothed and healthy as well.

Some of us may be called to take care of orphans, support those who are sick; others are called to be children's ministry teachers. Whatever way the Lord has called us, let's all do our part.

If your part that the Lord has called you to as a leader is making decisions that reflect the heart of Christ and connects children to

Jesus, His saving knowledge, love, and blessings, please do it, and do it well to the glory of God.

Whatever stage in life your children are, it is not too late to start covering them in prayer and in the Word. It is not too late to start mending relationships between children and parents. No matter how hopeless the situation may be, Jesus is not far from you; the destiny changer is not far from you. There are specific blessings that God has in store for children, but it takes the collective effort of the "village" to connect the kids to the heart of the heavenly Father. Let's join our efforts, prayers, and resources together and make it happen.

When we understand times & seasons, we will be moved to action.

Chapter 11

Understand the Times/Seasons

There are a lot of watchmen in the Bible. Their characters and stories are very unique, yet they hold some fundamental truths that bind them together. The central theme that runs through these three books in the Bible was men who sought to stand in the gap for the people of God so that God would act in favor of His people. They understood the times and seasons that they were in and what ought to happen for the people of God. And they were willing to engage God and His Word through prayer and practical action, and as a result, God brought a mighty deliverance to His people.

In the book of Daniel chapter 9, the most powerful and extraordinary prayer of Daniel was recorded. In verse two, the Bible says that during the first year of King Darius' reign, Daniel learned *from reading the Word of the Lord, as revealed to Jeremiah the prophet, that Jerusalem must lie desolate for seventy years.*

Daniel, being a man of the Word, discovered from the Word of the Lord that the season that he and his people were in was not a time to remain in captivity, was not a time to remain silent and do nothing, but rather a season of deliverance and restoration for the people of Jerusalem, the people of God.

By divine understanding, Daniel knew that something had to be done, and instead of resorting to blame and complaint, he went to the presence of the Lord to pray, to seek the face of the Lord, and to intercede for the people of God. He went looking for solution to the national problem at hand.

Why would Daniel do this? Because, for all you know, he was one of the high officials of the king in Babylon at this time, and so he could have decided not to do anything about it.

But because Daniel carried the heart of a watchman, he did not rest when the Lord revealed to him that deliverance and restoration were due unto Jerusalem at that moment in time.

Daniel could not rest on the issue because he had a heart of a true watchman, called and ordained by God. The truth is watchmen are problem solvers in the Kingdom of God. They are game changers in the Kingdom of God. They carry divine solutions from the Lord to the challenges that the children of God face. God, Himself, uses these men and women of God by His grace for His own divine agenda.

Watchmen see and perceive the things of God by divine revelation from the Word of God, from which they are led by the Spirit of God to take action and bring a divine solution.

When Daniel understood that the timing was right for God to move on behalf of his people, he went before the Lord, petitioned God, confessed his own sins and sins of the people of God, and pleaded on their behalf for the forgiveness of sins.

The prayer of Daniel was a remarkable prayer of humility! Daniel went before the Lord in the spirit of total humility. He did not distance himself from everyone else as someone who was more righteous than anybody else. He didn't also come to God to remind Him that he was the same Daniel God had saved from the lion's den. Daniel did not petition God on the basis of his uprightness before the Lord. He didn't come to throw certain people under the bus before the Lord while exalting himself above everybody else. He had no holier-than-thou attitude.

Instead, because Daniel was a true embodiment of who a spiritual watchman is, in his prayer, he actually reminded God of who He is, His covenant, and what His power is able to do. In other words, he gave full reverence and honor to the Lord and worshipped Him in his prayer. He fasted, put on sackcloth and ashes as a sign of humility, and petitioned God. After he confessed his own sin, the rest of his prayer before the Lord started with these two small letters in the alphabet and yet powerful word: *"We."*

Daniel 9:5–6 (NIV) says, *"We* have sinned and done wrong. *We* have been wicked and have rebelled; we have turned away from your commands and laws. *We* have not listened to your servants the prophets, who spoke in your name to our kings, our princes and our ancestors, and to all the people of the land," and he continues the rest of his prayers to God in this manner.

The posture of the heart of Daniel was that of total humility before God.

Watchmen have a heart of humility that allows them to identify with the needs of others.

The intercession of Daniel on behalf of the people of God drew the attention of God in heaven and His heavenly hosts. No wonder God, in His mercy, sent the angel Gabriel to deliver a response to Daniel's prayers.

As we learn to be the watchmen that God has called and anointed in any sphere of life, let's learn to have spiritual ears to hear the Word from the Lord, the authentic Word of the Lord, go before the presence of the Lord, and intercede for others, for our families, nation, with a heart of humility and also compassion.

Anyone without Christ is a person whose walls are broken.

Chapter 12

The Game Changers

...and I asked them concerning the Jews that had escaped,
which were left of the captivity, and concerning Jerusalem.
Nehemiah 1:2b (KJV)

There are people who sometimes ask you how you are doing not because they truly care about your personal well-being, but some ask for the sheer niceness of it. Others ask out of courtesy, and there are also those who ask for the sake of gossip. Just so they will hear something new from you that they can carry out to share with others. Oftentimes this group cannot keep a single secret about anything, and so they casually talk about issues you deem personal.

But then there is another group of people who don't just ask you how you are doing. These kinds of people are different, and what makes them different is the fact that they truly care. They have a big heart, a true sense of purity and compassion, and willingness to be of help no matter what you're going through. These are the kind who will cry with you and also laugh with you. In other words, people who don't mind rolling up their sleeves, giving you a listening ear, and going far and beyond for you.

Whereas some other people may often exploit and take advantage of your kindness, true watchmen are sent by God into our everyday lives to carry the agenda of God. Such was Nehemiah. And so even though he was a cupbearer in Susa serving the Persian king in those days, we can pretty much say that he was in the king's palace and a place of comfort as compared to some of his brothers and sisters.

Yet he did not allow his comfort to put him in a place of complacency, arrogance, or spiritual pride; rather, he genuinely asked about the welfare of his Jewish brothers and sisters who escaped the captivity of the king and were not exiled and also about Jerusalem as a whole.

Nehemiah asked because he cared. Not only did he care for the well-being of his people, but he also knew who he was and what God would be able to accomplish through him. Nehemiah was a watchman; he was the man who carried the hope of the Jews and the city of Jerusalem at that time. He carried the answer to the prayers the people of God believed God for. And to some who even felt like there was no possibility of restoration, he spoke life and hope and reminded them of who their God was and His track record of His mercy and faithfulness to His children.

Nehemiah sought to know how the people of God were doing because he knew he carried the grace and power to intercede for the people of God. Not only that but because he knew that God had the power to use him to deliver solutions to the people of God, to help build and restore the broken walls of Jerusalem. He knew that God had embedded in him the grace and power to restore the children of Israel's hope and trust in the Lord again, restore holiness and allegiance to the Lord again, and bring the people back to repentance, obedience, and spiritual alignment again.

And so when Nehemiah learned that the walls of Jerusalem were broken, he did not rejoice and did not entertain any blame game. Neither did he exalt himself above the people of God to tell them he was better than them. Rather as a true watchman, he went to God in his secret place of prayer and fasting to seek for the mercy and help of God. His prayer pattern followed the same as Daniel's. He acknowledged the greatness of God, confessed his sin and the sin of the children of God, and asked for the favor of God before the king he was serving so that he would allow him to go back to his country and help build the broken walls of Jerusalem (Nehemiah 1:3–10).

Because of the gracious hand of the Lord that was upon the life of Nehemiah, God granted his requests, and the king supplied every need he had for rebuilding the walls of Jerusalem. No matter the challenges Nehemiah and the children of Israel faced, they trusted in the Lord and rebuilt the broken walls of Jerusalem.

The success of this story started with just *one man* who genuinely asked how his people were doing one day.

Nehemiah's "ordinary" inquiry led to the restoration of a whole generation, returning to God in holiness, and the glory of God being restored.

Nehemiah did not receive an angelic visitation like Daniel, but he had confidence in the prayers he prayed that day to the Lord and was confidently assured of God's help to rebuild the walls.

Sometimes we wait so much, looking for God in some supernatural way, maybe a voice from heaven calling out our name, or sometimes even through a dream or our familiar way that God speaks to us. But you see, sometimes God chooses to reveal His greatest assignments, His will, or approval of something He wants us to do through the ordinary things in our lives.

May the Lord help us not to miss His voice, His visitation, in our day, our time when He comes speaking to us through our everyday things. May we have ears to hear, eyes to see, and feet to go where He has ordained for us to go so that through His grace, we can accomplish exploits in His kingdom.

The truth be told, we all have broken walls that need to be restored. The broken walls signify a city whose people are no longer under the protection of the almighty God. Consequently, they are susceptible to all kinds of attacks from the enemy. They have no place of refuge or defense. When your walls are broken, it means you're spiritually disconnected from the Lord, and in our dispensation, you are eternally disconnected from the Lord. The spiritual wall that affords you the eternal protection from being eternally separated or disconnected from God is Christ alone.

Not only does the Lord Jesus Christ have the power to cover us through His blood while we are on earth, but He also ensures our safety to heaven. Not only do we have hope, peace, and love here on earth, but we have eternal life, unconditional love, and a living hope in God.

Anyone without Christ is a person whose walls are broken.

God is looking out for true spiritual watchmen who will be willing to say to God in this end time, "God, show me how I can rise and start connecting broken vessels unto You. How can I join in the building of the broken walls of people I come across daily? How can I be a conduit of hope, love, and peace around me? How can I be a *salt and light* where You have placed me?" God needs the church to rise and say, "Lord, show us what you want us to see, hear, and do so that we can pass on what we have received from the Lord unto others can be spiritually restored unto your Kingdom."

God is calling out to the Nehemiahs who are passionate about bringing forth a change, who aren't just leaders who sit on the fence and dish out instructions but rather practically roll up their sleeves and join in the actual work. Leaders who are relatable, humble, and inspire others for exploits for the Kingdom of God. Let's rise up and help build the Kingdom, not religious church silos, for time is not on our side. Let our everyday lives draw others to the love of God and saving knowledge of Christ. Let us be intentional about preaching sound messages from Scripture that draw others to Christ rather than to ourselves and to a specific denominational "church."

The master key to the gates of the *Lord* is a heart of *thanksgiving*.

Chapter 13

Watchmen and Gates

Gates are entry points into our lives, hearts, minds, and destinies of people and nations. Just as physical gates cannot be left ajar without the proper security, similarly, our spiritual gates need to be guarded also. The lack thereof leads to spiritual casualties in homes, schools, government, the marketplace, and every sphere of life.

Gates also represent a place where decisions are taken, whether good or bad. Gates are very important.

The Gates of the *Lord*

Before we touch on any other form of gate, we must first know how to enter through the gates of the *Lord.*

"Enter into his *gates* with *thanksgiving,* and into *his courts* with *praise*: be thankful unto him, and bless his name" (Psalm 100:4, KJV).

Gates are entry points; gates can be locked or opened. The best way to access the presence of the *Lord* is to come through the gates of the *Lord.* We cannot possess the rest of the gates without first coming through this particular gate. The *password* to this gate is "*thanksgiving.*" The master key to the gates of the *Lord* is a heart of "*thanksgiving.*"

Watchmen need to have a heart of gratitude that often overflows with thanksgiving and a sense of appreciation. Thanksgiving prepares and ensures that the posture of our hearts is right before the *Lord.* It takes the focus off us and shifts all of us to focus on God. Thanksgiving brings us to our knees, to a place of humility where we give credit to the God who holds our very lives in His hands. When we sincerely begin to thank God, we lose all our pride, and honor the almighty God who has given us the gift of the *breath* of life for each day, strength, the ability to walk, talk, see, touch, taste, eat, a roof over our heads, food, the daily miracles of life that we take for granted.

Our thanksgiving to God shouldn't just be when things are going well, but rather a daily thing regardless of whether we have all of our needs met or not, whether happy or sad. We should never enter into the presence of the *Lord* without thanksgiving.

A heart of gratitude full of thanksgiving amplifies and multiplies the provision of God. Jesus understood this revelation, and therefore, He demonstrated it while here on earth. This is the reason why before the Lord Jesus Christ will do any miracle, He will always give *thanks to God first*. No matter how impossible the situation looked, He entered the gates of the *Lord* with the right attitude, with the right posture of heart.

Before He performed the miracle of feeding 5,000 and more with five loaves of bread and two fishes, He *first gave thanks*. Before raising Lazarus back to life after being dead for four days, Jesus *first gave thanks*.

As watchmen called and positioned by God, we need to cultivate this attitude of *thanksgiving* also. Only God knows the miracles in store for us if we will begin to enter the gates of the Most High God with the powerful keys of giving sincere thanks unto the Lord.

Guarding the Gates of Life

True watchmen, true soldiers of the cross, are needed in this end time to stand guard at the spiritual gates of our lives.

There are individual spiritual gates that allow you to be equipped and function properly at the geographical gates or gates tied to a particular place of assignment.

Whether we acknowledge it or not, every individual has spiritual gates, and they consist of the *eye gates, the ear gate, the mouth gate, and, the biggest of all, the mind gate (mental).*

These gates are directly connected to your body, the temple of the Holy Spirit, and so I call them the *"temple gates."*

> *Do you not know that your bodies are temples of the Holy*
> *Spirit, who is in you, whom you have received from God?*
> *You are not your own; you were bought at a price. There-*
> *fore, honor God with your bodies.*
>
> 1 Corinthians 6:19–20 (NIV)

The temple gates aren't just connected to us physiologically, psychologically or emotionally. They are actually gateways to our spiritual life. These gates allow us to connect spiritually with the heavenly Father. Through our temple gates, we accept Christ into our lives or reject Christ. *"That if thou shalt confess with thy mouth the Lord Jesus, and shalt believe in thine heart that God hath raised him from the dead, thou shalt be saved"* (Romans 10:9, KJV).

What you do with your temple gates matters a lot as a believer.

We need to be careful of what we *use our eyes to see, ears to hear, mouths to say*, and of course, what we allow into our *minds (mentally)*. These are powerful gates that, if we don't make a conscious effort to allow the Holy Spirit of God to be in control of these gates, we can wreck our very own lives and other people's destinies.

We fellowship and encounter God through these spiritual gateways. We study the Word, worship, and pray through these gateways.

What results from our encounter and fellowship with God through our temple gates becomes the launchpad of our ministrations. Before we can occupy the geographical or territorial gates, we need to first allow the Holy Spirit to possess the temple gates. This is where we can properly *hear, see, speak, conceptualize and visualize through our minds or imaginations, and then through the divine power of the Holy Spirit*. We can possess these *gates* literally.

The Geographical or Territorial Gates Are Connected to Influence and Territories

Some of these gates are gates to your home, family, social media, the government, marketplace/workplace, or place of assignment. God has divinely and strategically positioned some of us in places where we find ourselves today for a far greater purpose than we think.

We are not randomly at the places we find ourselves. No, we are divinely positioned there as servants of the Most High God, endowed with supernatural mantles of watchmen, ambassadors of Christ, who are on a Kingdom assignment for God, and so, therefore, we take our orders from God and His Word alone.

Gates to your home: Every home has gates and doors. The gates of our homes are the initial link between the external world and everything we have in our homes. The gates connect people or things to come in from outside and inside. Gates give us primary access to doors leading to rooms and treasures in a home. If the gates are not secured, anybody can come in and easily access what belongs to you.

The truth is none of us goes to bed leaving gates to our homes and the doors of our precious homes unlocked. If we consistently and consciously make sure that our homes are fully secured from intruders physically, what makes us think we can leave the spiritual gates and doors of our homes unsecured?

Our homes need to be eternally secured, with the gift of life that endures forever and ever. We need to be connected spiritually to the ultimate life-giver, the Lord Jesus Christ. Without Him, no one will see God or have access to God. The gift of salvation is the fundamental access to making sure that members of our household are eternally secured. The gift of salvation is the ultimate gate that connects us and gives us keys to access doors to Kingdom treasures, authority, power, and grace. The gate of salvation opens our eyes, ears, hearts, and minds and unveils our depraved nature, our need for repentance, and the full access to grace of God, the righteousness of God, the love of God, and the treasures of the Kingdom of God.

We need spiritual watchmen in our homes who will arise during these end times, lead your family to Christ, and sow prayer and the Word of God into lives of members of our household. We need parents who will not let a day pass by without making sure that their children are eternally connected and secured in the Word/prayer, in holiness, clothed with the love of God, and spiritually fortified.

Preach the unadulterated Word of God. Most important of all these is the practical application of the Word, being intentional about walking in love and extending grace to everyone in the home. We need to be the walking Jesus in our homes. Parents, children, grandmothers/grandfathers, uncles, and aunties, everyone needs to take their rightful positions at the home gates.

If all we are exposing our kids to in our homes are video games and the latest tech gadgets, we are doing more harm than good spiritually. If all we are working so hard to give our children is the best education without first giving them Christ, we are leaving them spiritually empty and spiritually exposed to all the deceptions of this world.

Now more than ever, we need fathers to wake up and stand as spiritual watchmen at the gates of their homes. We need our fathers to rise up in the righteousness of Christ and ensure that their families are secured and built on the solid rock of Christ. We need our fathers to rise up as true watchmen of the Kingdom, living out Kingdom principles in their homes and leaving positive and eternal legacies for their children.

Marketplace/workplace gates: We may have physical bosses in our workplaces, but our overall boss is God Himself. We do whatever we do with the highest level of integrity, and excellence, because we answer to a higher authority greater than anybody on earth. As a result, we set higher standards for ourselves. We need to operate as Kingdom men and women. We don't need to talk just like everybody else because our lips are anointed by God. We have the tongue of the wise. We have life and death in the power of our tongues. We decree and declare the powerful Word of God, and it becomes established!

Spiritual watchmen in the marketplace need to be consciously looking for ways and opportunities for others to make Christ known. Because we are set apart for the Lord, we preach first through our character, attitude, work ethics, and, of course, our words. We don't do mediocre work. Our standards are higher; therefore, by the wisdom of the Holy Spirit, we become problem solvers and provide solutions to challenges.

We are bearers of the Gospel, the good news of Christ. We preach repentance from sins, the salvation message encapsulated in the great grace and the relentless love of God constantly reaching out and pursuing humanity! Every one of us preaches Christ and Him crucified and His second coming. We are on divine assignment in the marketplace, and we need to rise up to our callings right where we are. Some souls that need to be saved in the marketplaces are tied to our obedience. God may have put us in close proximity to someone from work who may be depressed, suicidal, sick, or in need of help for whatever reason so that we can rise up and point them to Christ.

Media gates: The media gates are so powerful in our world today. They come in various avenues, such as television, radio or airwaves, and social media platforms. The media gates essentially influence our everyday lives now more than ever, and they are connected to our *eye gates, ear gates, and mental gates.*

Watchmen need to be at the media gates, or we will be drastically impacted by them.

God has called us to possess the gates of our enemies. The enemy for us is nobody but the devil himself! His influence and indoctrination at these gates cannot be overlooked. The negative impact of the media affects both young and old, rich or poor.

On the flip side, the positive impact of the use of the media to spread the Gospel across the globe is revolutionary!

We need more watchmen who carry the authentic message of the Kingdom of God to possess the gates of the media and be willing to release the end-time prophetic messages to the church and the world. The true message of repentance, righteousness, peace, and hope.

According to resource marketer, social media use in 2019 were as follows:

- South America spends three hours and twenty-nine minutes.
- People in Europe spend an average of one hour and fifty-three minutes on social media.
- North Americans use social media for around two hours and six minutes daily.
- In Asia, the usage of social media is two hours and sixteen minutes daily.
- Africans utilize social media for three hours and ten minutes a day.

The above research results were from 2019, and so with interference of the pandemic in our daily lives in 2020, it is with no doubt that we've been forced to rely on technology in unprecedented ways to enable us to function and accomplish our everyday tasks more effectively. Consequently, I believe the rate of use for each country around the globe has definitely skyrocketed.

And so whether we want it or not, the social media gates are wide open, easily accessible twenty-four seven. There are so many positives as well as negatives. It all depends on how much we will make a conscious effort to regulate our individual use of it, and make sure we are channeling it towards the right purpose, and also the wisdom to restrict our use.

The temptation to be addicted to social media is real, but thanks be to God that His grace is available through the Lord Jesus Christ to help us avoid all extremes. I have personally had to do social media fast a couple of times, just to remind myself once again that I can live life and operate without it, and then also to apply myself to some discipline in the use of my time wisely.

We need spiritual watchmen to be the gatekeepers who mandate *who* and *what* gets to enter our homes to either add eternal value to our lives or not. If, for any reason, we know that the *who/what* is not serving any eternal purpose, we stand in divine authority with the sword of the spirit, which is the Word of God, and prayer and let it go. This is the season when we need discernment to shut the gates to some of the deceptions the enemy has packaged and branded nicely but deceptively for us. Evidently, this will help us embrace and make room for what the Lord has ordained and destined for us to accomplish through the leading of the Holy Spirit.

We need to avoid anything that steals our time and makes us inefficient and unproductive. Avoid any enticement to sin against the Lord.

Because if there is any agenda that the devil has for children of God, it is only the same old, same old agenda to come *steal, kill, and destroy*. And he does it in subtle ways sometimes. But thanks be to God, who gives us the victory through our Lord Jesus Christ.

The Gospel message is an *urgent message*. When a generation loses this sense of *urgency* attached to the Gospel message, we become a lukewarm generation!

Chapter 14

Preach the Gospel

In 1 Corinthians 9:16, the Apostle Paul says, "For if I preach the Gospel, that gives me no ground for boasting. For necessity is laid upon me. Woe to me if I do not preach the Gospel!"

Sounding the trumpet of the Gospel is every believer's responsibility. To Apostle Paul, it was a necessity, and he further assumed a personal burden and trouble if he failed in this important but urgent task.

To him, it was his duty, and he took it personal and did the best that he possibly could.

The spiritual watchmen of today need to take the preaching of the Gospel seriously, like the Apostle Paul. We must understand the true meaning of the Gospel and attach a greater sense of urgency and significance to it.

If there was a time the Gospel message needed to be preached and heard, that time is now. That season is now when the coming of the Lord is evidently at hand.

If there was a time we needed to sound the alarm of the Gospel to the whole world, that time is now more than ever.

The Gospel message is an *urgent message*. When a generation loses this sense of *urgency* attached to the Gospel message, we become a lukewarm generation!

The early church preached Christ with the blazing fire of the Holy Spirit! Nothing could quench this blazing fire, no wonder they preached till some died in all manner of painful deaths. These were the great Apostle Paul, Peter, James, Stephen, etc.

Throughout the church history, we have seen, heard, and read of some of our great fathers/mothers in the faith who heralded the Gospel message with the same level of *urgency* and fire.

This is our time to rise up! With the same fire of the Holy Spirit in our bones and *urgency* to preach the Word! Will the true *authentic* ministers of the Gospel arise in this end time and be counted among the Lord's army?

Will the true Holy Ghost firebrand young men and women with the gift of influence in the marketplaces and social media platform gates arise and reach out to others with the Gospel message instead of merely chasing fame, likes, following, and money?

I pray the Lord will cause a spiritual awakening in all of us and let us know we've all been called for such a time as this to be part of the Kingdom agenda. Everything can't just be about the "self." We represent the Kingdom of God.

There is a *One* True
God, Creator of heaven
and earth, whom *all*
men and women are
accountable to.

Chapter 15

The Coming of the King

A king or a president never comes to a place or an event without a special announcement. Therefore, before Lord Jesus Christ came to be born as a human being, prophecies upon prophecies went ahead of His birth. Why? Because He wasn't just any human being, He was the King of kings and the Lord of lords, a member of the Godhead/ Trinity; therefore, He couldn't just come to earth without a proper introduction or announcement.

In the same way, if He is to return back on earth to take His bride—which is the church—home, then there must be people who will also announce His coming back.

The Bible is full of the announcement of the Second Coming of Christ. The signs to look out for, the events that will take place, and so many others.

Perhaps the Apostle John's revelations give us a more vivid account than any other writer in the Bible.

Believers are the watchmen who need to be at the spiritual gates at any sphere of life so that we can announce the coming of only the King of kings and Lord of lords. The lion from the tribe of Judah!

Revelations 22:12 (KJV) says, *"Behold, I come quickly..."*

The day and the hour we do not know, but for sure, He is coming quickly!

We must be ready to meet Him. We must be ready to be judged also. Whether someone believes this or not, the truth of the matter is Jesus Christ is coming. Your personal opinions won't change this. *There is a one true God, creator of heaven and earth, whom all men and women are accountable to.*

Jesus Christ is Lord, the only way to God. He is coming soon. May we announce His love, heart, and passion for every soul, even if that soul is just you or me.

> *Be dressed for service and keep your lamps burning, as though you were waiting for your master to return from the wedding feast. Then you will be ready to open the door and let him in the moment he arrives and knocks. The servants who are ready and waiting for his return will be rewarded. I tell you the truth, he himself will seat them, put on an apron, and serve them as they sit and eat! He may come in the middle of the night or just before dawn. But whenever he comes, he will reward the servants who are ready.*
>
> *Understand this: If a homeowner knew exactly when a burglar was coming, he would not permit his house to be broken into. You also must be ready all the time, for the Son of Man will come when least expected.*

Luke 12:35–40

May we announce that this is the hour of *grace*, beckoning to every lost and weary soul for true rest.

May we announce that the justice of God allows Him to bring everybody to the judgment seat to be judged based on what we did while on earth.

May we announce also the *mercy* of God, which speaks for us through the precious blood of the Lamb of God, is available to everyone.

We need spiritual watchmen in every sphere of life, where we can effect change with an elevated mindset.

Chapter 16

Watchmen Need to Be in the "Palace"

All through the Bible, there were great men and women of God, such as Joseph, Mordecai, and Esther, who had to be at the gates and also transitioned into the palace, where they assumed another dimension of influence. This is where these watchmen had a mindset shift, and therefore they were able to influence the lives of many others for the sake of the Kingdom of God.

The palace level is where we legislate and rewrite laws. This is where we solve national and global problems.

When Joseph—though a prisoner yet a man of excellence, integrity, and full of the fear of the Lord—was called to the palace to interpret the dream of the Pharaoh, he changed history!

The Spirit of the Lord released global-level solutions unto him that preserved lives in Egypt and beyond.

Joseph moved from the prison rooms and gates to the palace, where he became a prime minister. A watchman of a godly influence!

In the same way, Mordechai once upon a time used to be at the gates where a man called Haman demanded of him to bow before him, which by his loyalty to the Living God, he refused to do so. But when Mordechai was promoted to the palace as a high official, he nullified the handwritings of Haman and rewrote the laws that favored the people of God.

Haman was finally dethroned as a high official when Queen Esther wisely, prayerfully, and strategically broke the palace protocols to seek an audience with the king.

Watchmen are needed to be in our palaces today. We need watchmen in every arena, in every place of influence where we can effect change.

This palace sphere of influence is where we operate with an elevated mindset!

"And God raised us up with Christ and seated us with him in the heavenly realms in Christ Jesus" (Ephesians 2:6, NIV).

Watchmen who operate with the palace-level mindset know their spiritual identity as royals! We operate with the highest level of authority and jurisdiction in heaven and on earth. We rule and legislate through the highest level of power embodied in the name of Jesus Christ, the name that is above all names, power, and principalities both in heaven and on earth. Every territorial influence bows to the name of Jesus Christ! We war on our knees with weapons that are not carnal but mighty to the pulling down of strongholds. We war through prayer, Word, praise and worship, holiness, love, fasting, giving, and the complete armor of God.

Watchmen operate at the frequency of the power of the Holy Spirit! This is the dimension that we can step into and can then speak to dry bones and dead situations to come back to life.

Until we preach the true Gospel of Jesus Christ, His birth, death, resurrection, Second Coming, and salvation of souls, we have no moral right to demand that signs and wonders shall follow us!

God doesn't just do miracles, signs, and wonders to show off or please us. He does it so others will believe in the Gospel. He performs miracles so others can come and believe in Him. Too many times, the reason why we believe God for a miracle is just so we can show off, not to bring God the glory. When the posture of our hearts is right, we will see God manifest His sovereign power in greater dimensions.

Spiritual watchmen, until we rise and hear from God, preach the true Gospel, call sin what it is, seek for repentance, preach godliness and holiness, preach and practice the love of God, and extend grace, mercy, and forgiveness to those who have hurt us, we will not experience God and His power to the level He intends for us to.

Jesus said this to His disciples before He left to heaven:

> *Go into all the world and preach the Gospel to all creation. Whoever believes and is baptized will be saved, but whoever does not believe will be condemned. And these signs will accompany those who believe: In my name they will drive out demons; they will speak in new tongues; they will pick up snakes with their hands; and when they drink deadly poison, it will not hurt them at all; they will place their hands on sick people, and they will get well.*
>
> Mark 16:15–18 (NIV)

We cannot quote Ezekiel chapter 37 and begin to call forth dry bones to become as flesh until we have first practiced Ezekiel 3:17. Our true mandates as spiritual watchmen start from here. This is where we first have an intense fellowship with God. This is where we tarry in the presence of the Lord. This is where we study the Word, fast, hunger, and thirst for God. This is where we encounter the power of the Holy Ghost. This is the place and season we hear from the Lord, receive divine revelations from the Lord, and give warning about repentance to people. We speak the oracles of God. This is where we preach holiness. This is where we preach in season and out of season.

After we have boldly preached the true Gospel, we can then begin to step into the realm of the full manifestation of Ezekiel's chapter 37 experience. This is where we have the moral right and authority and power to partner with the Spirit of the sovereign Lord to call forth the dry bones to become flesh.

Until believers of today rise up and preach the authentic gospel message to all creation, certain dimensions of signs and wonders will not accompany the church, those who believe.

Watchmen, may we rise today with power, authority, and a sense of urgency and contend for souls. May we be set ablaze with the fire of the Holy Spirit and the Word of God! Revival of the church is here. May the true watchmen of God wake up and take our place at the gates and at the palaces!

God bless you!

References

https://www.kidpik.com/blog/kids-clothes-budget

https://review42.com/how-much-time-do-people-spend-on-social-
    media/